My Traveling Toddler Coloring Book

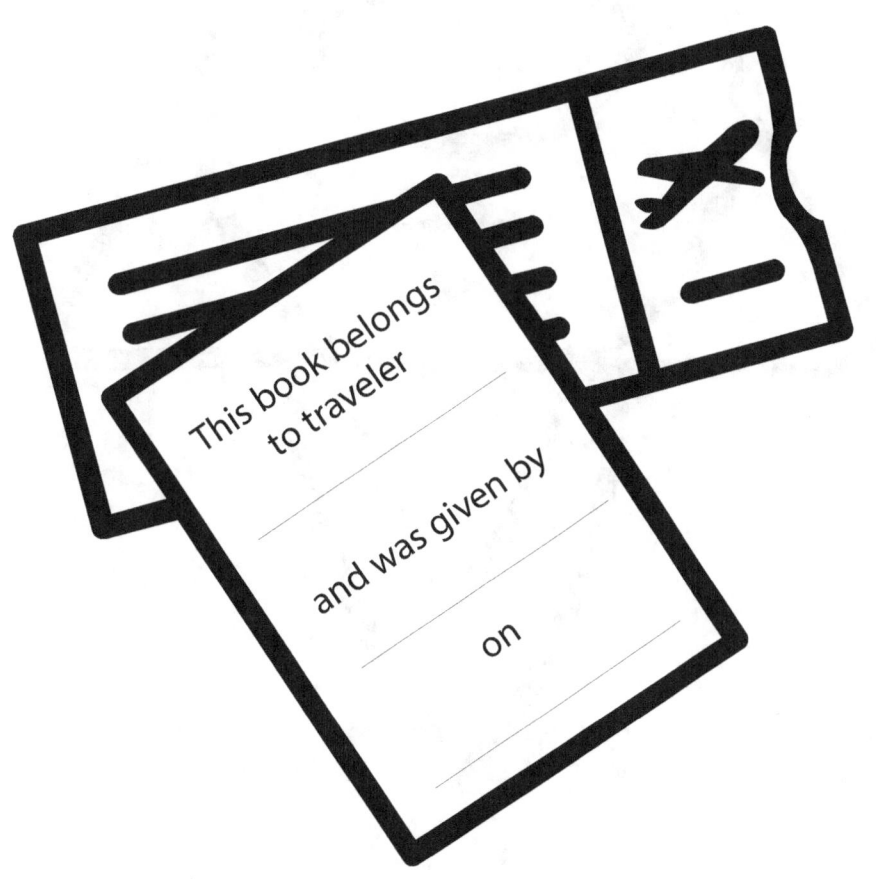

This book belongs to traveler

and was given by

on

Zoom around the

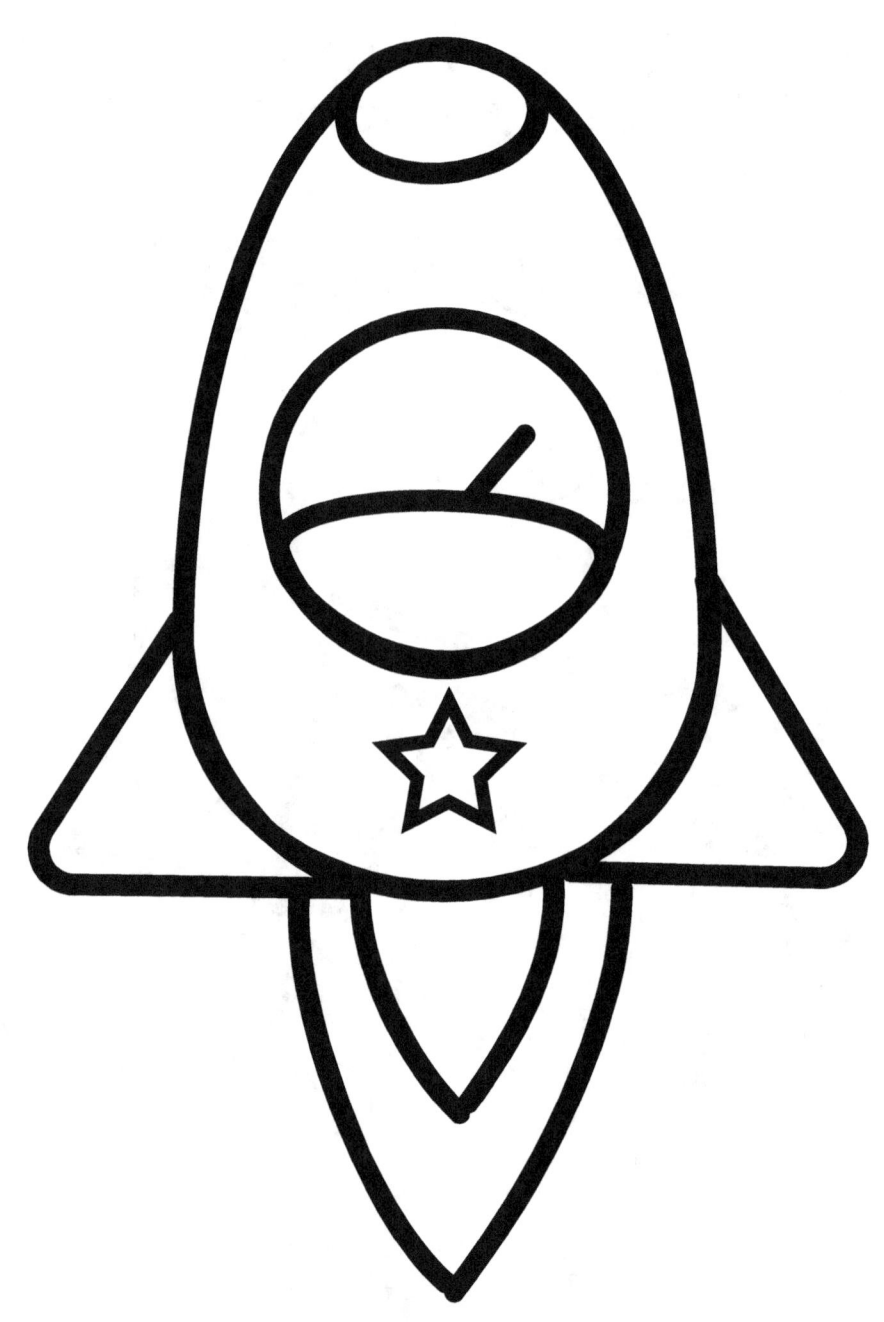

MOON!

Booked & Ready

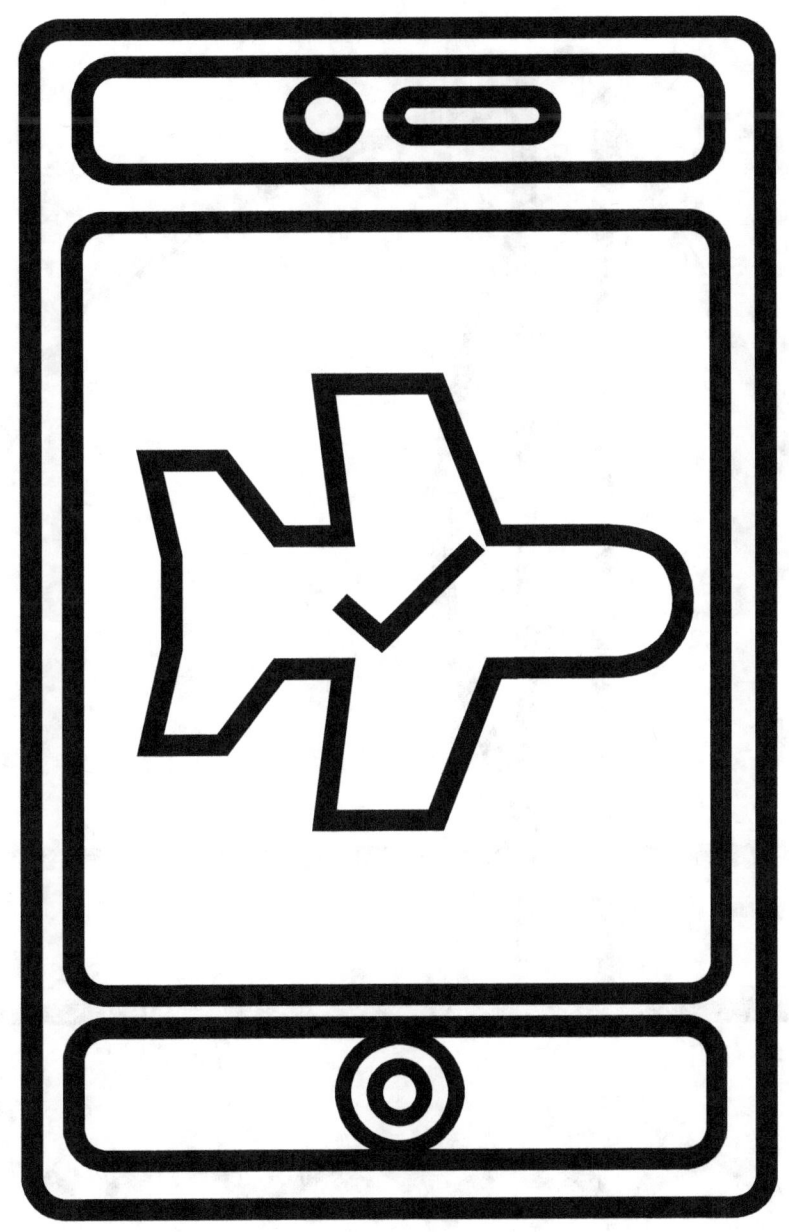

TO TRAVEL!

Sailing the ocean

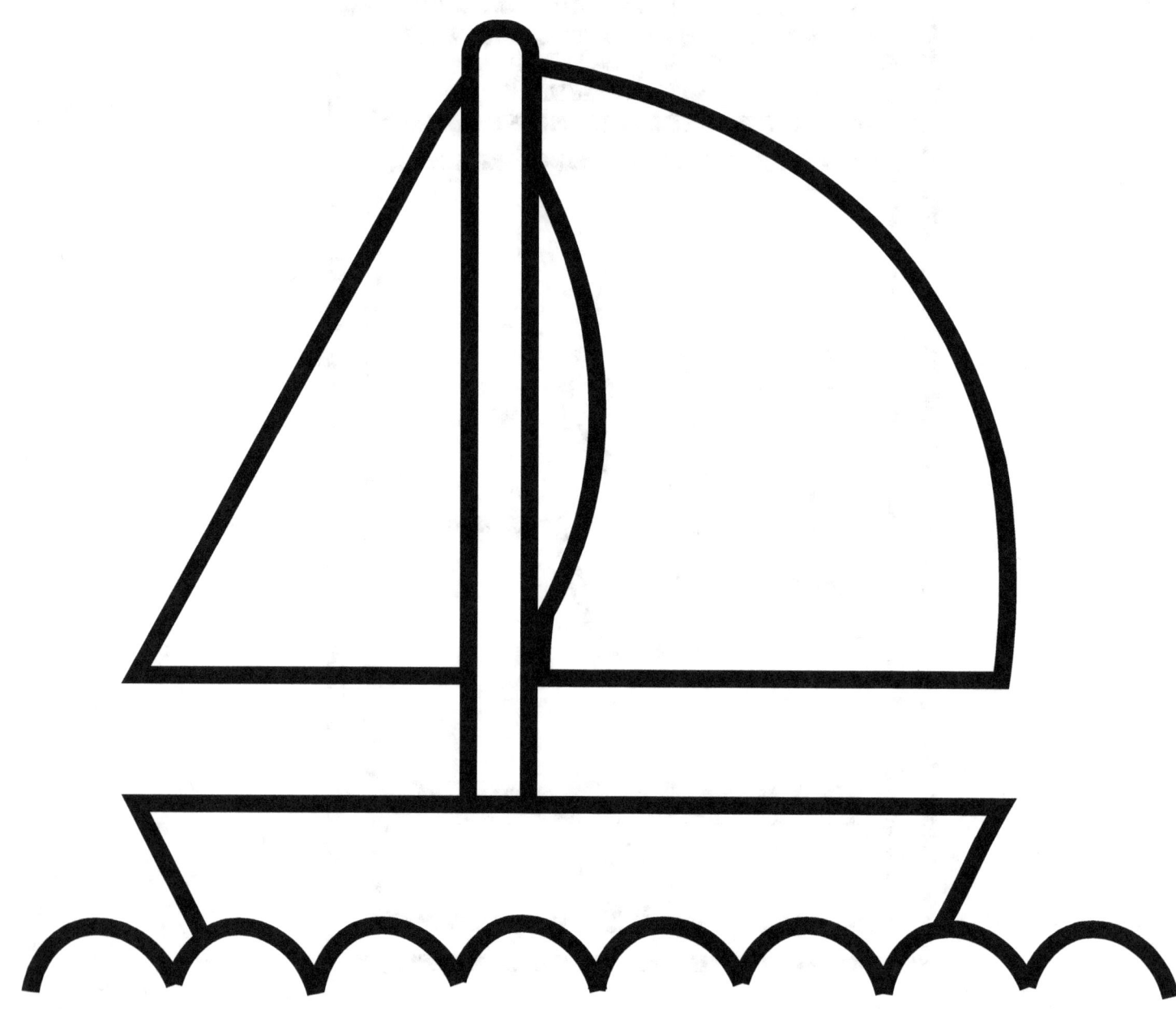

BLUE!

A good night's

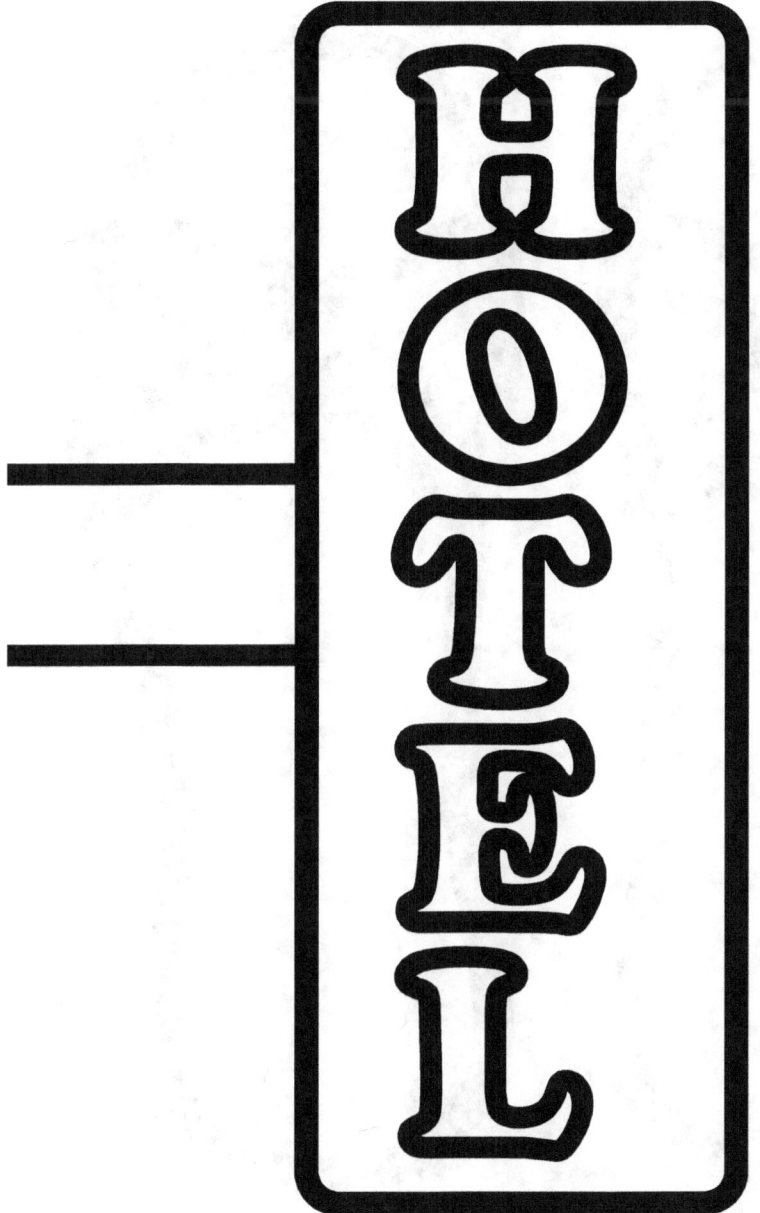

SLEEP!

Sandals + Beach

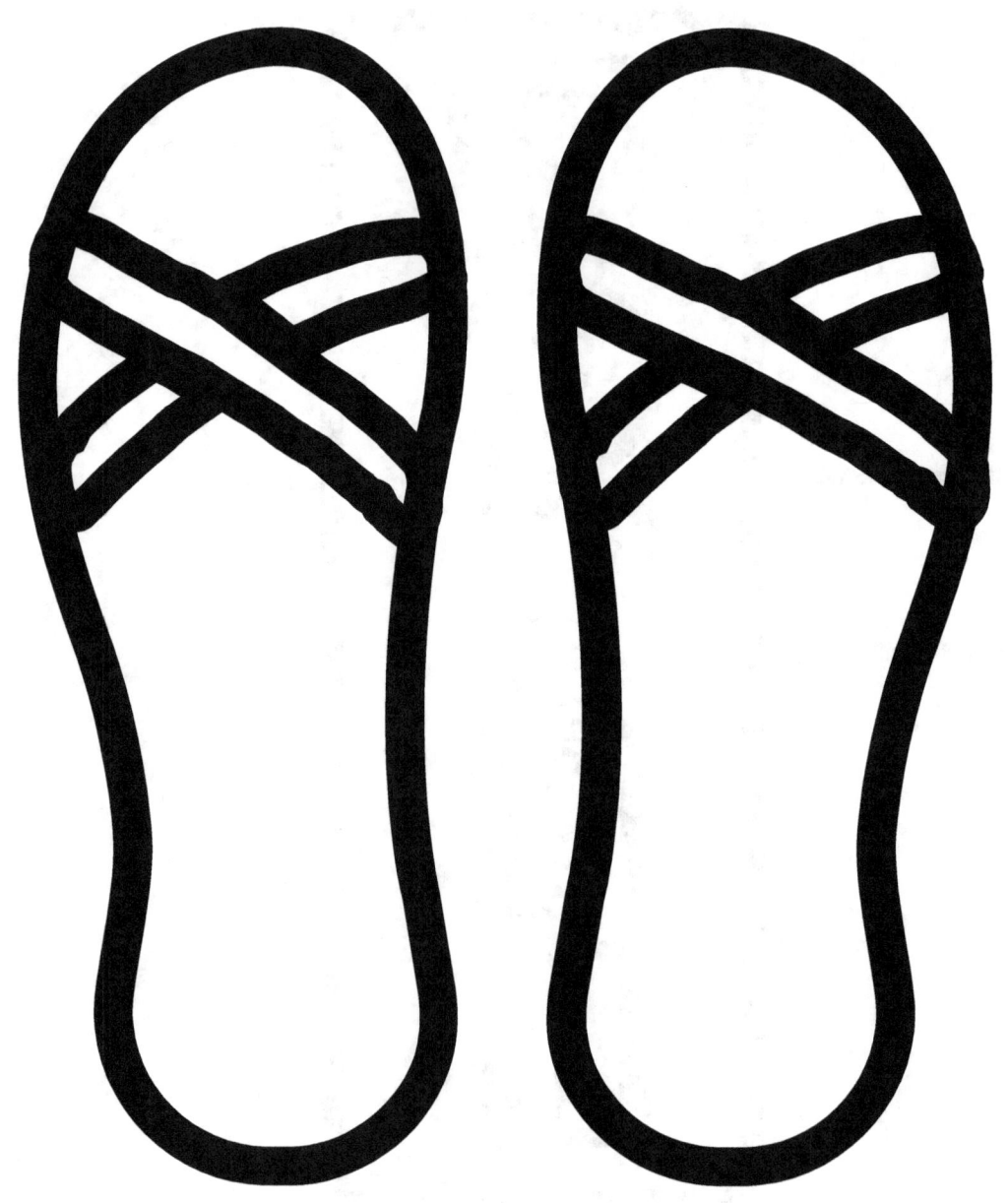

= LIFE!

Love this

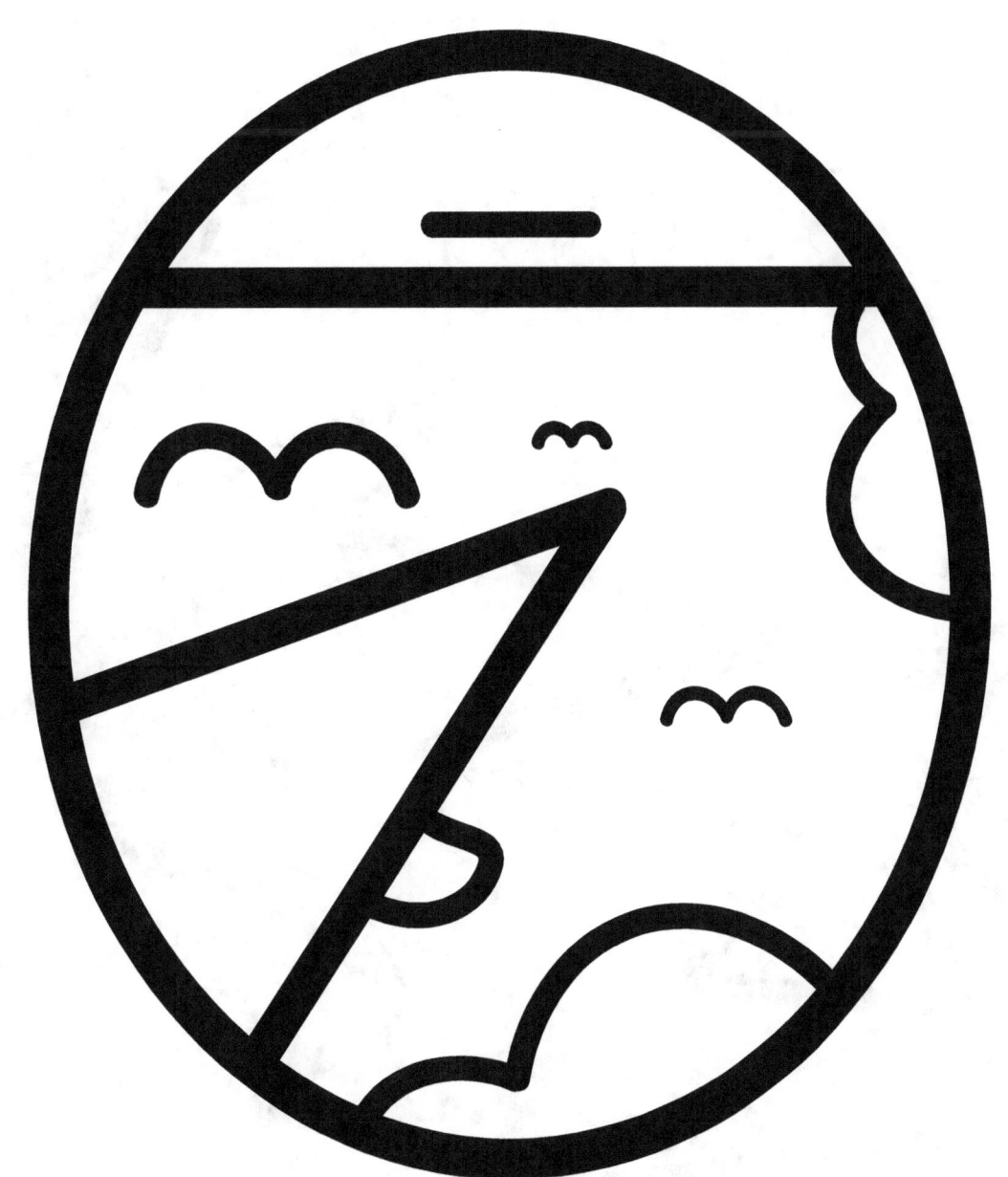

VIEW!

From Point A

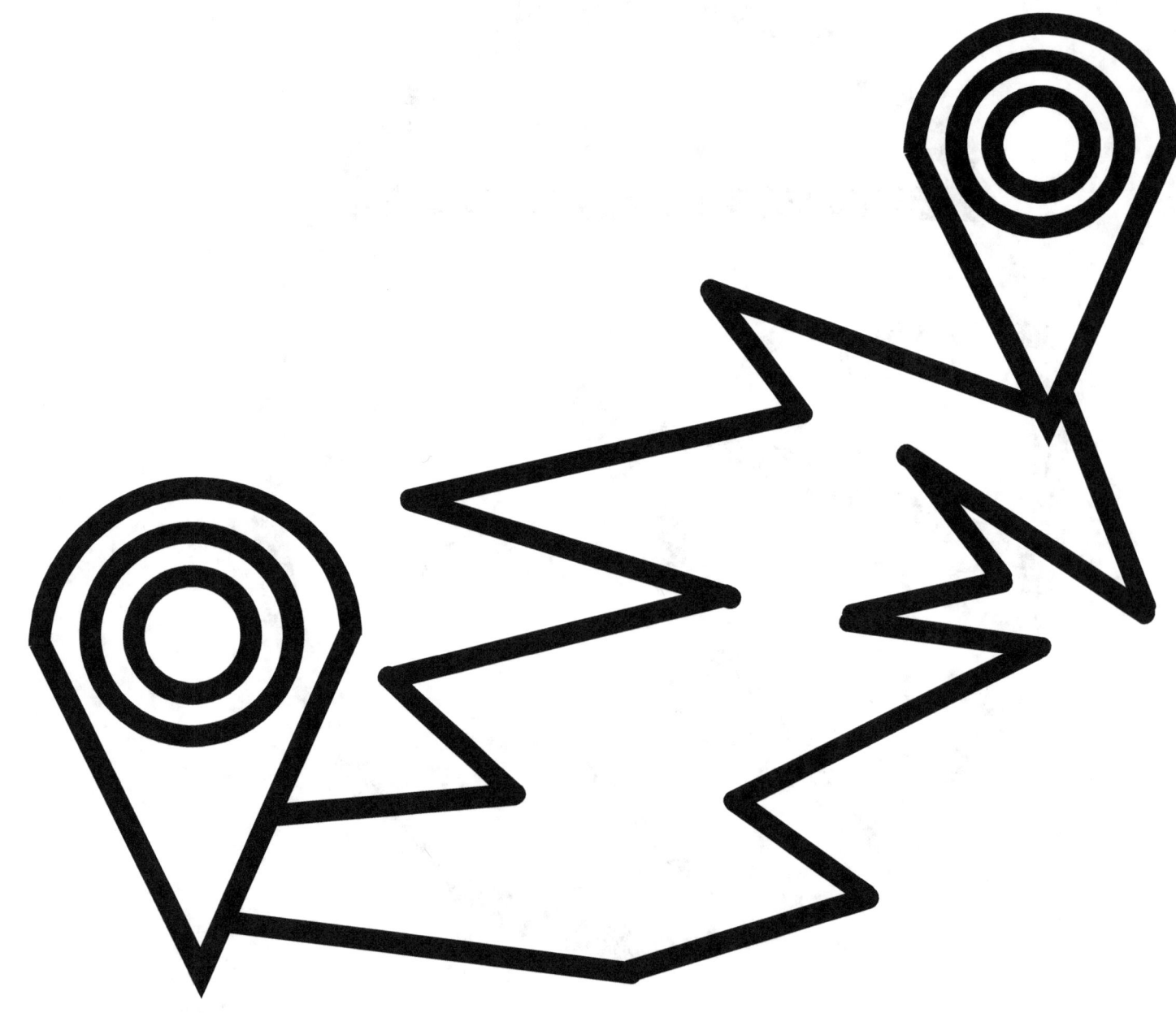

TO B!

Swimming

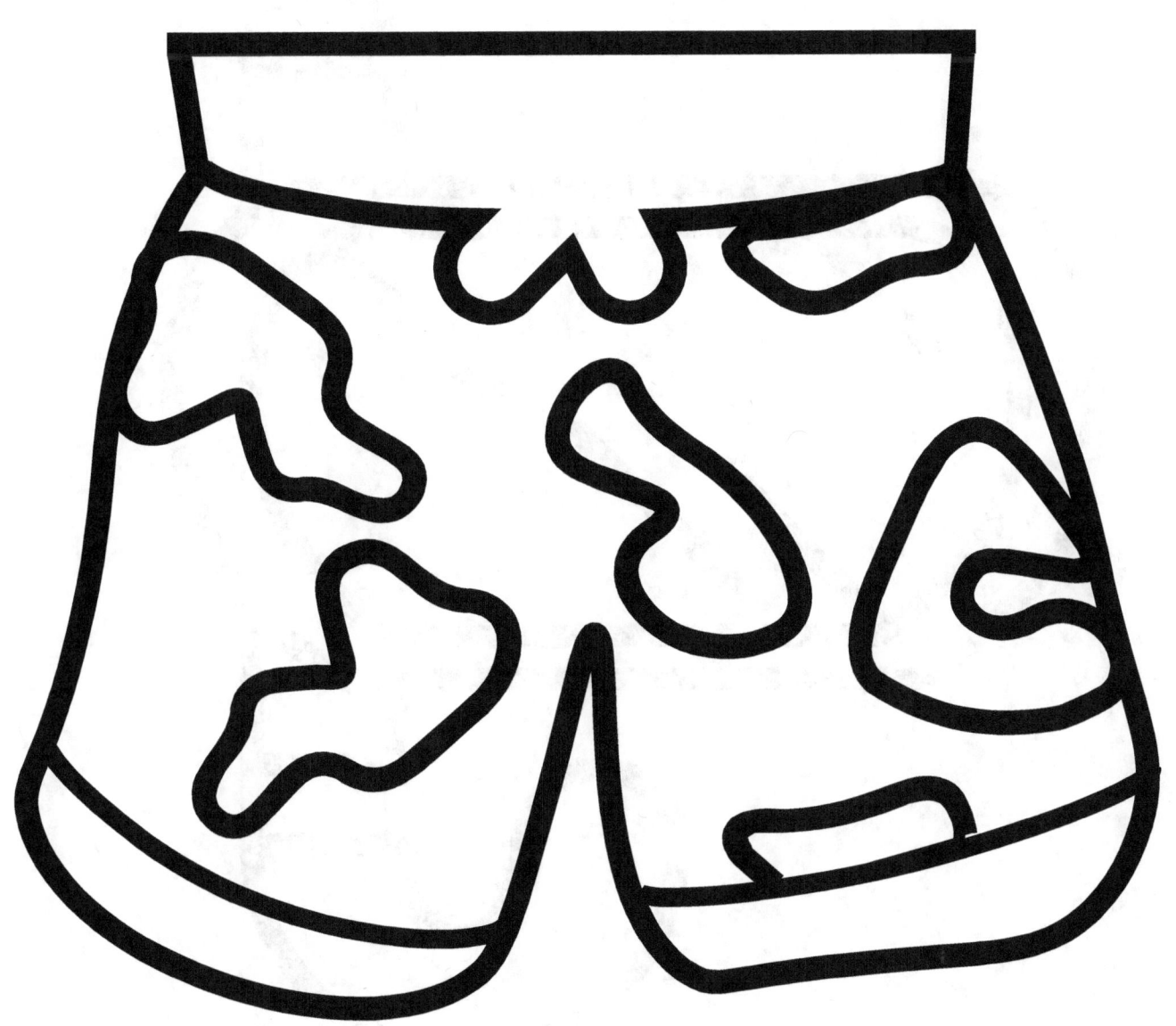

FUN!

Under the

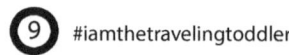

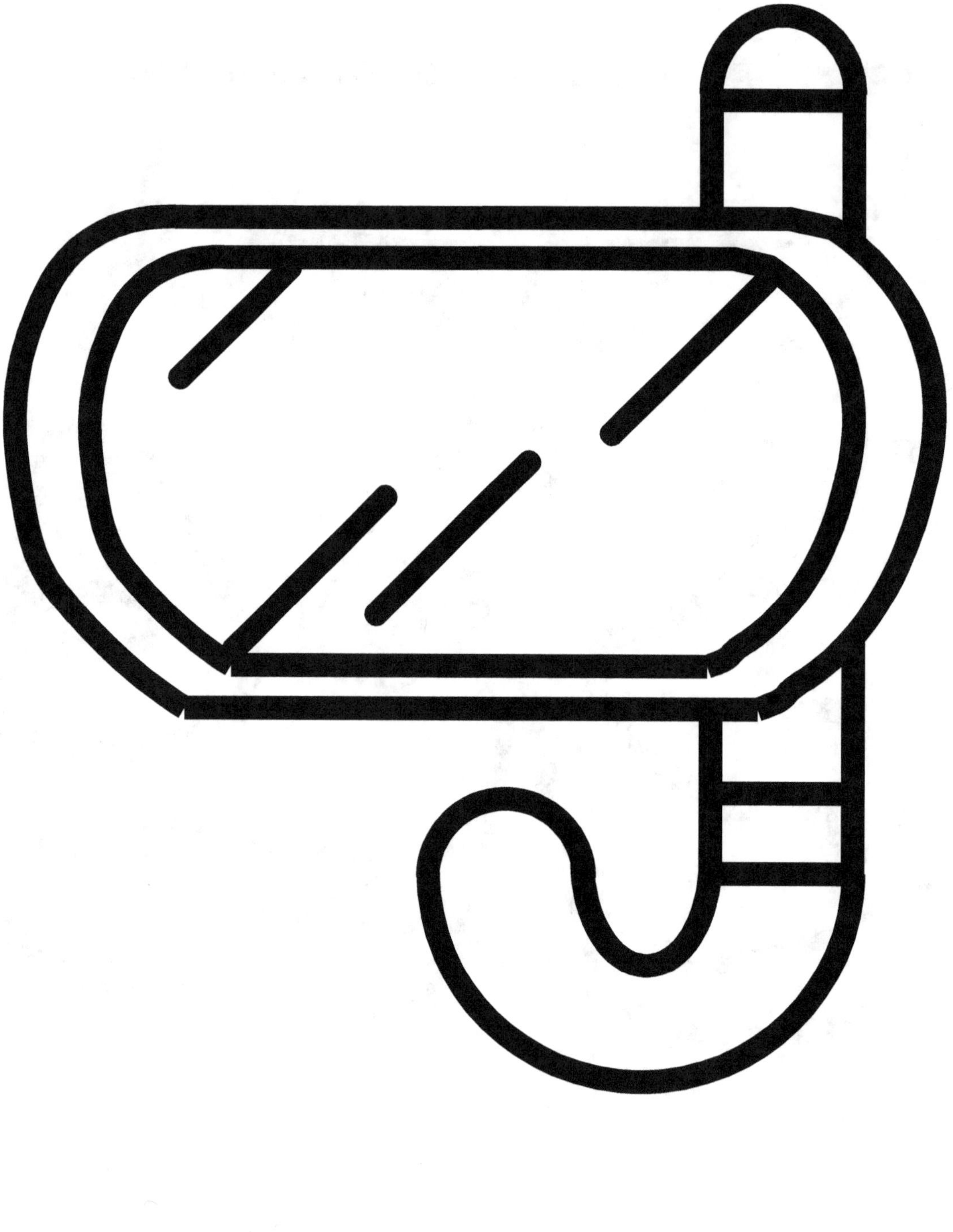

SEA FUN!

New Country to

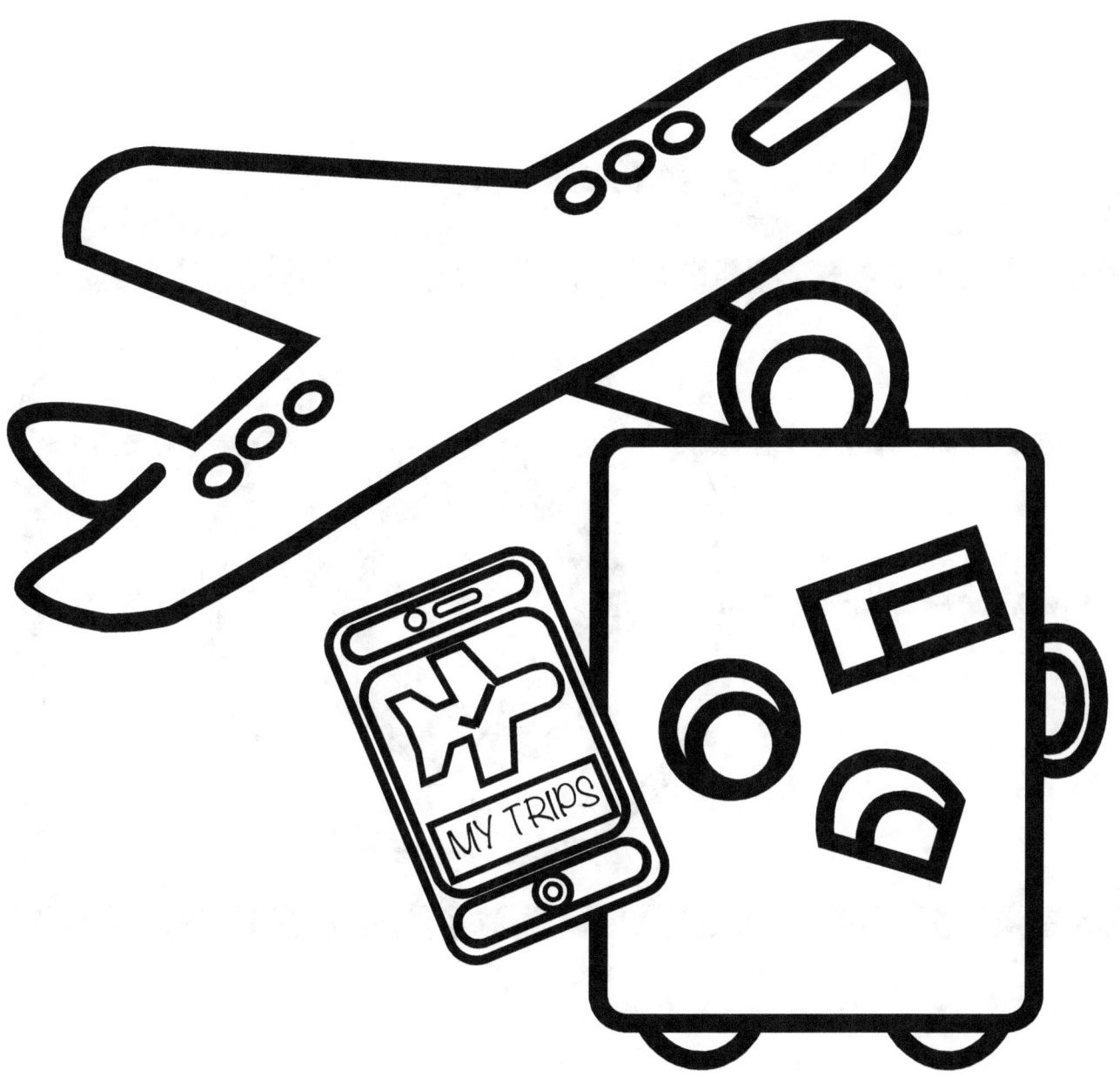

SEE!

1, 2, 3,

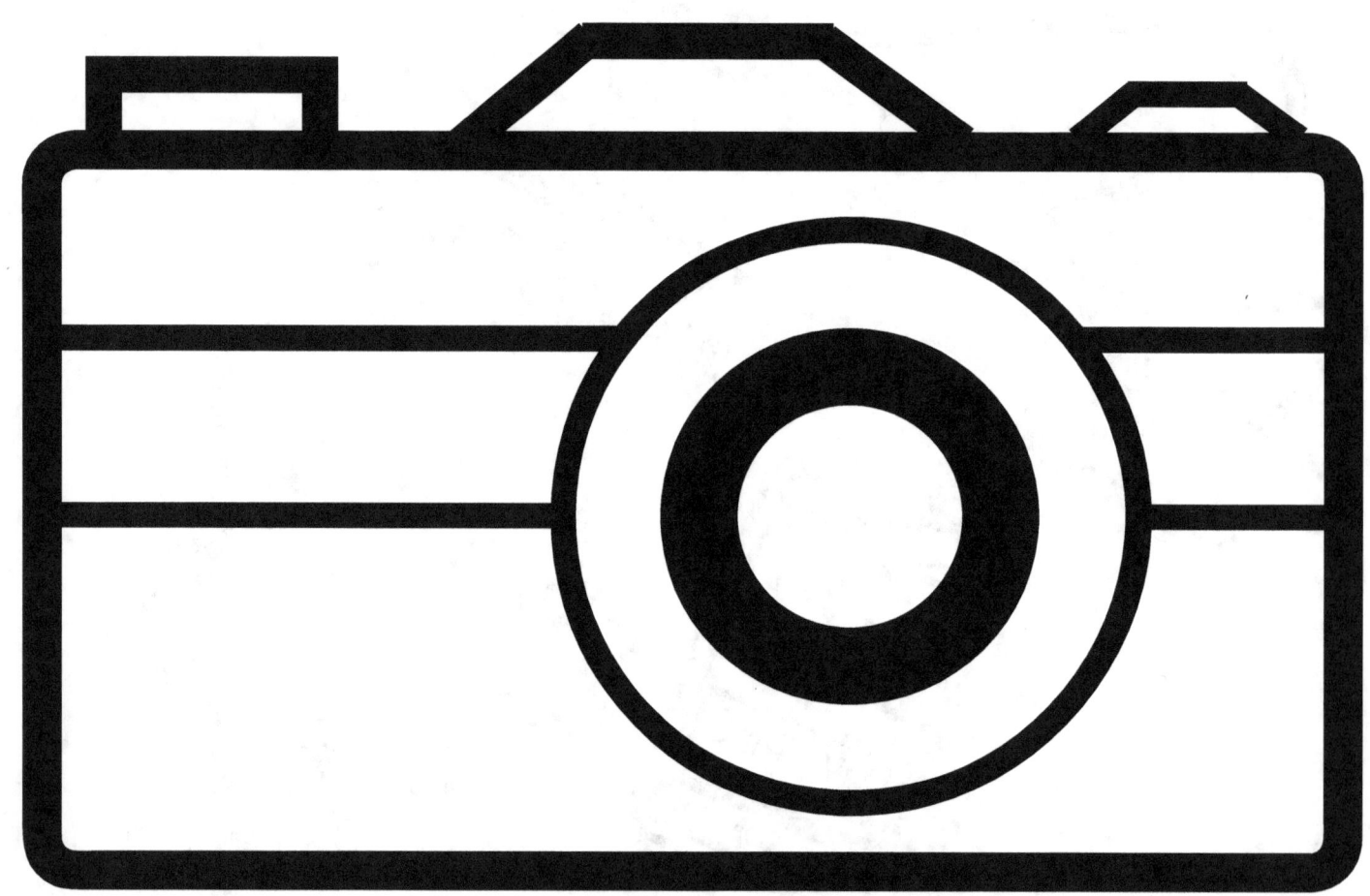

CHEESE!

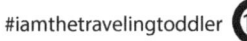

Passport Stamp

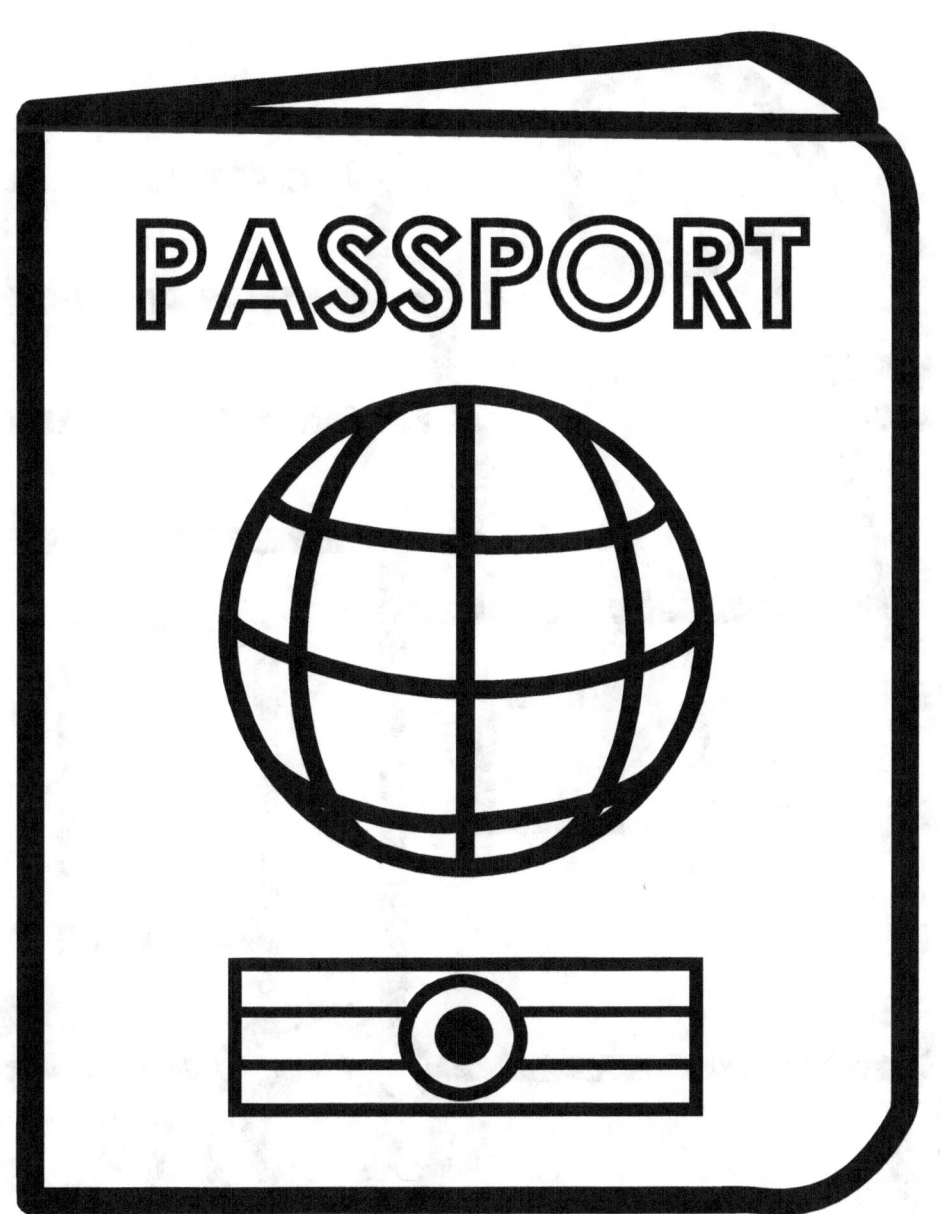

PLEASE!

Choo-Choo

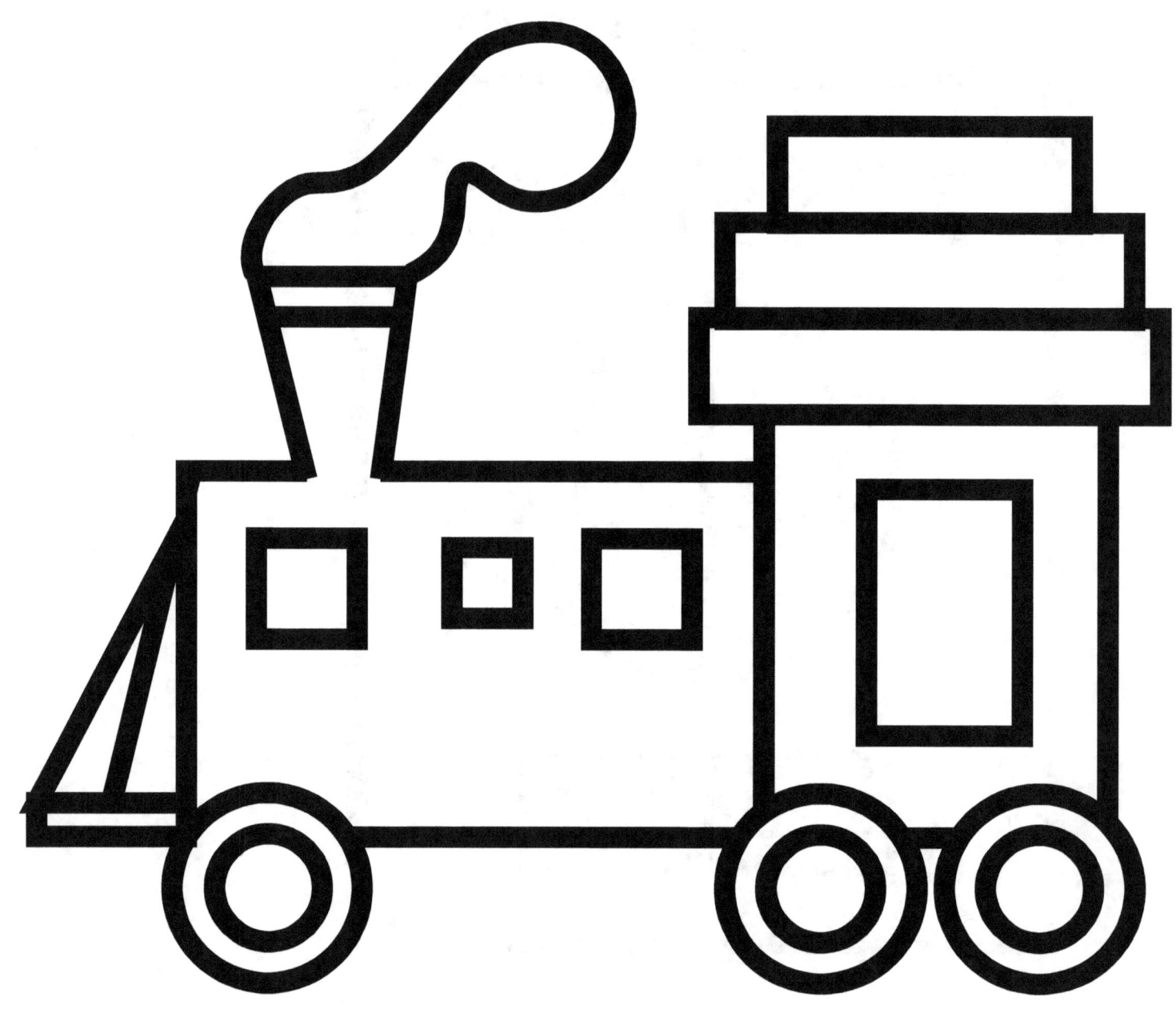

TRAIN!

Our Room

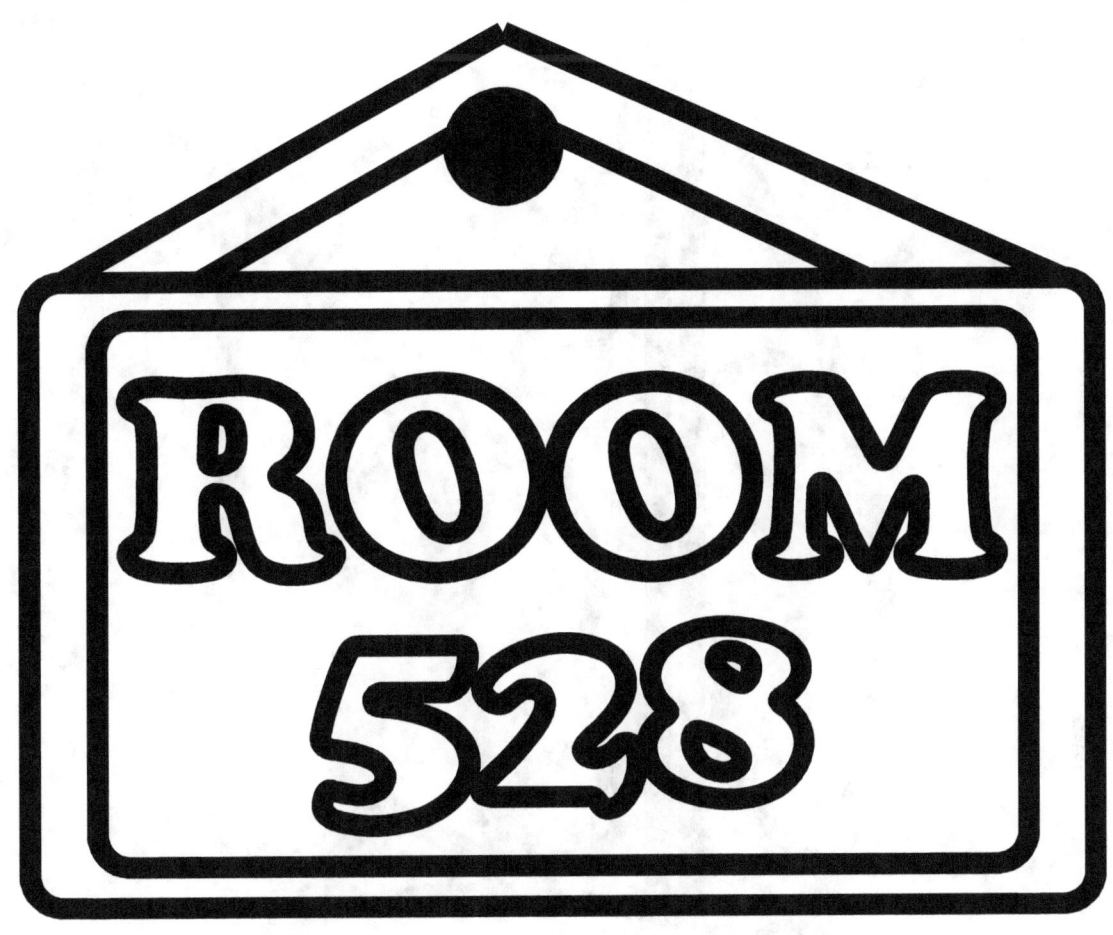

PLEASE!

Surfs

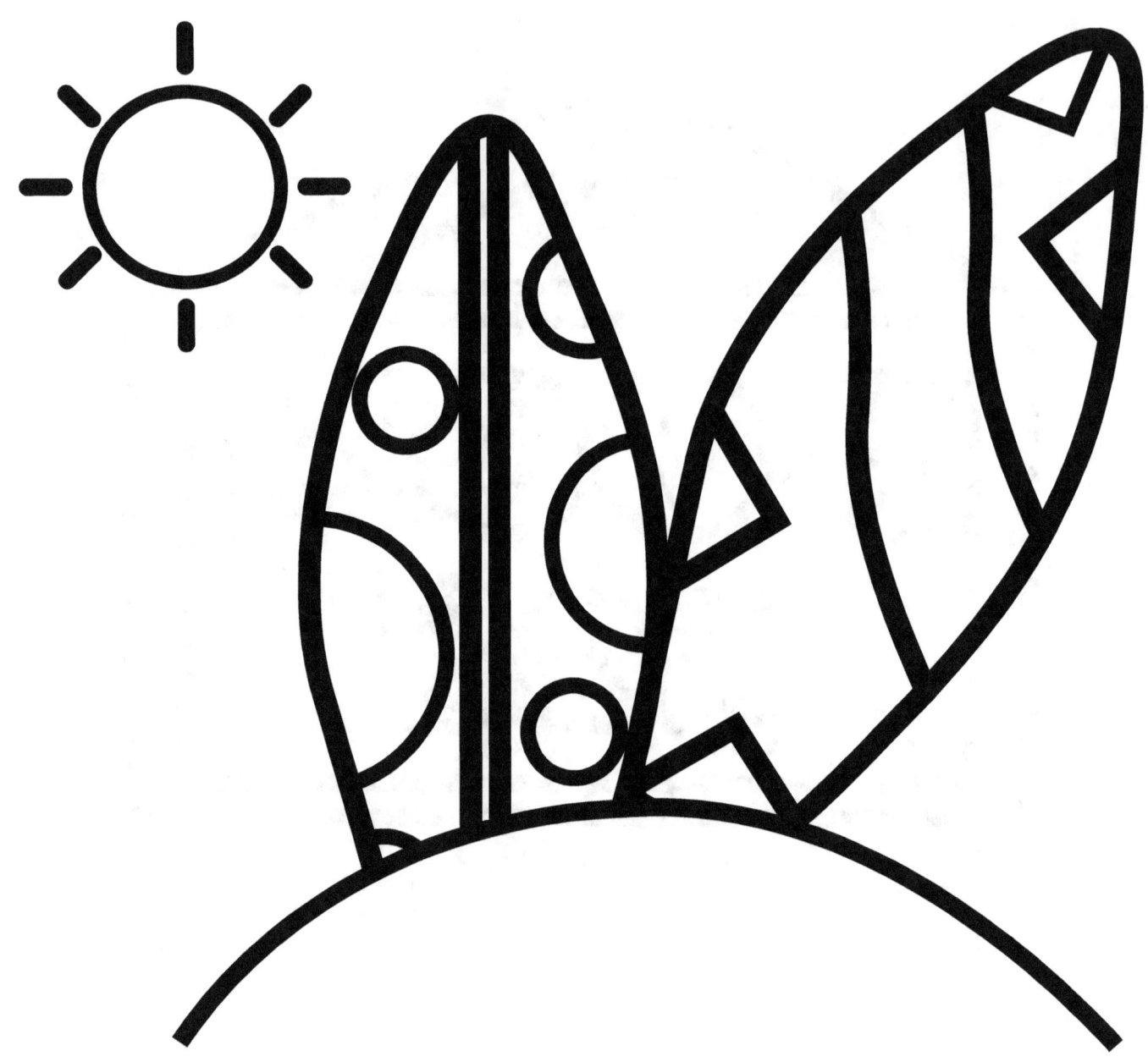

UP!

Up, Up, and

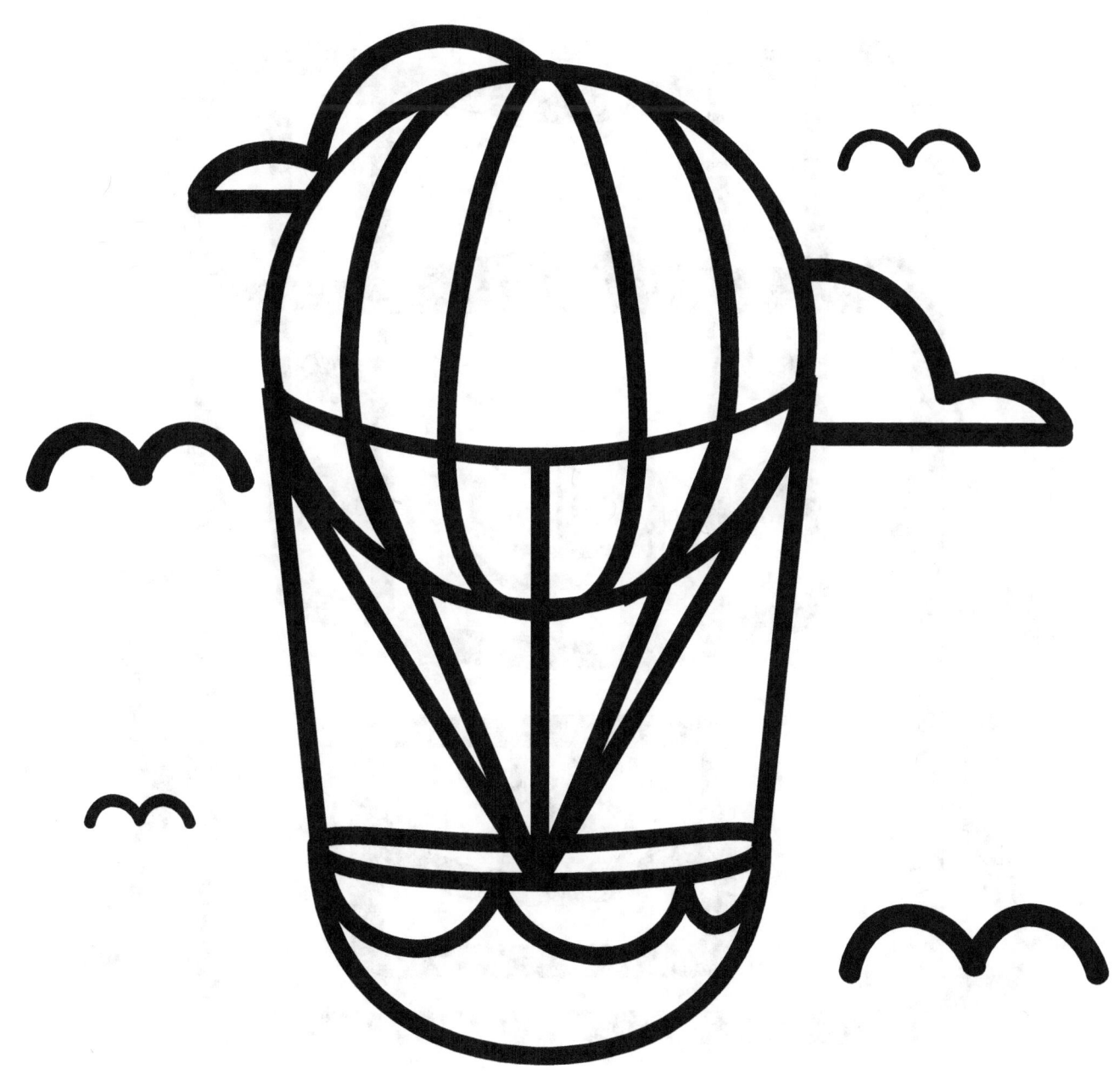

Away!

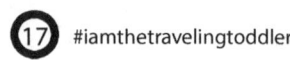

Backpack

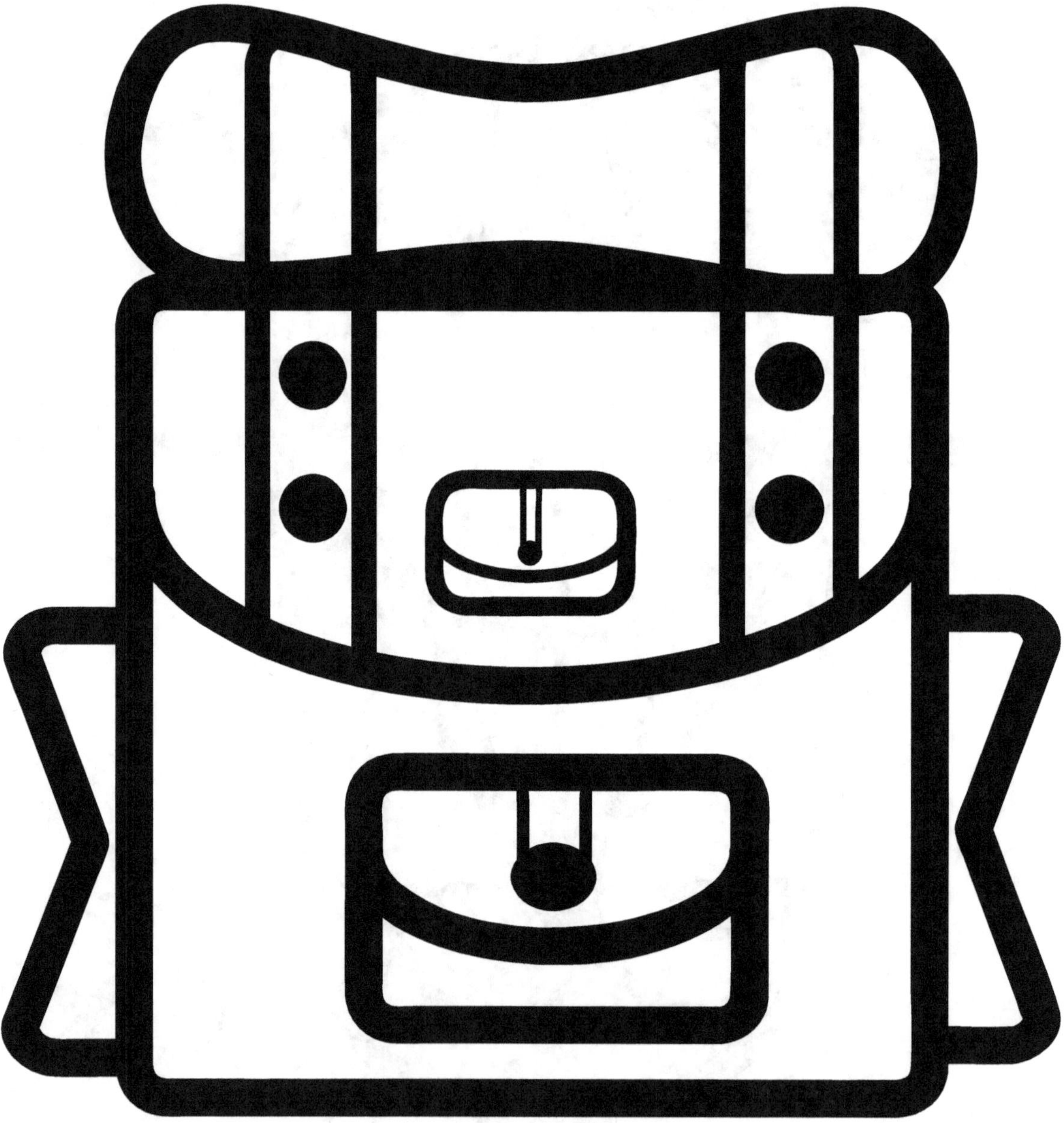

READY!

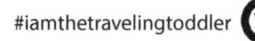

Beautiful Sea

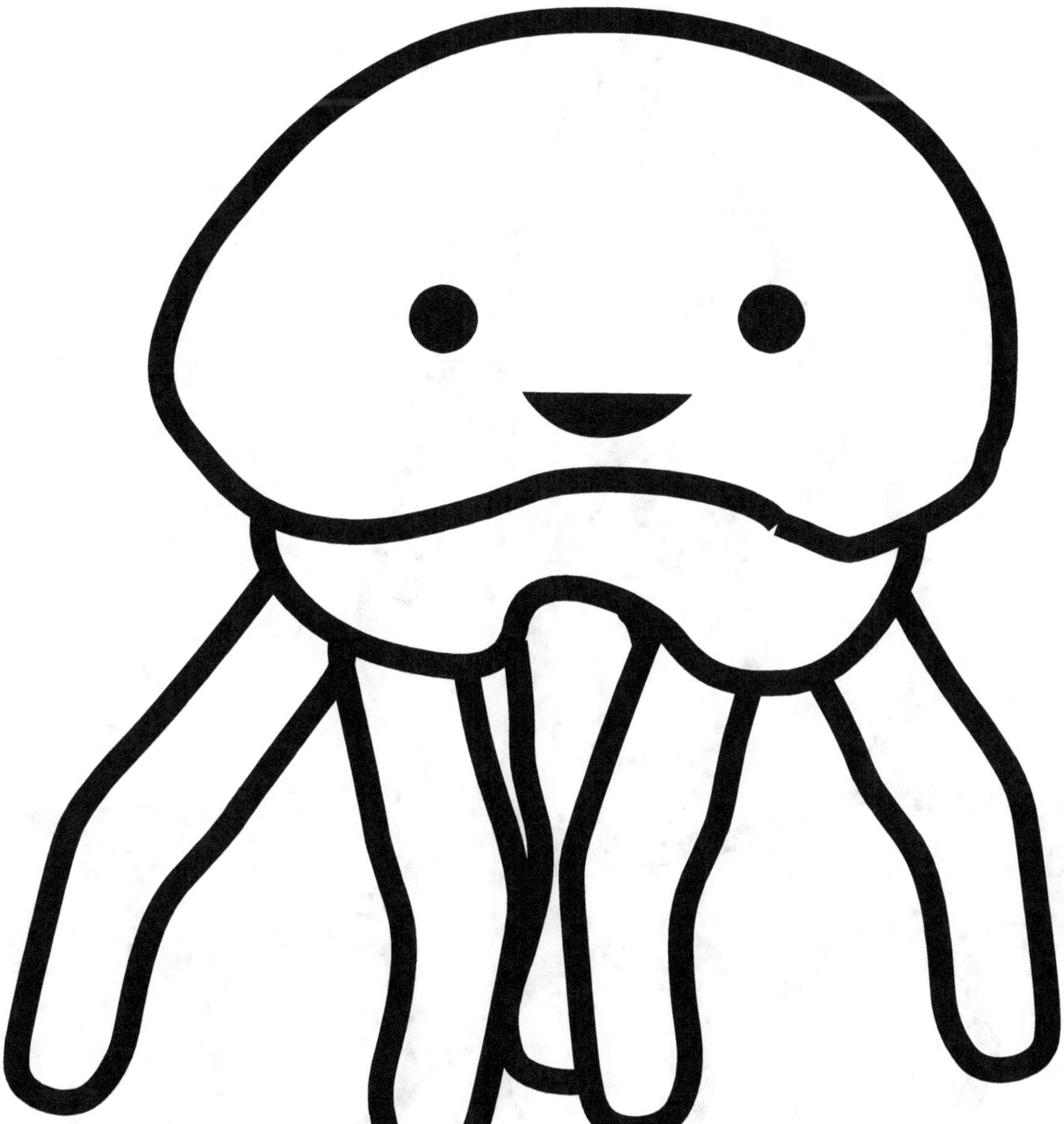

FRIENDS!

Camping is

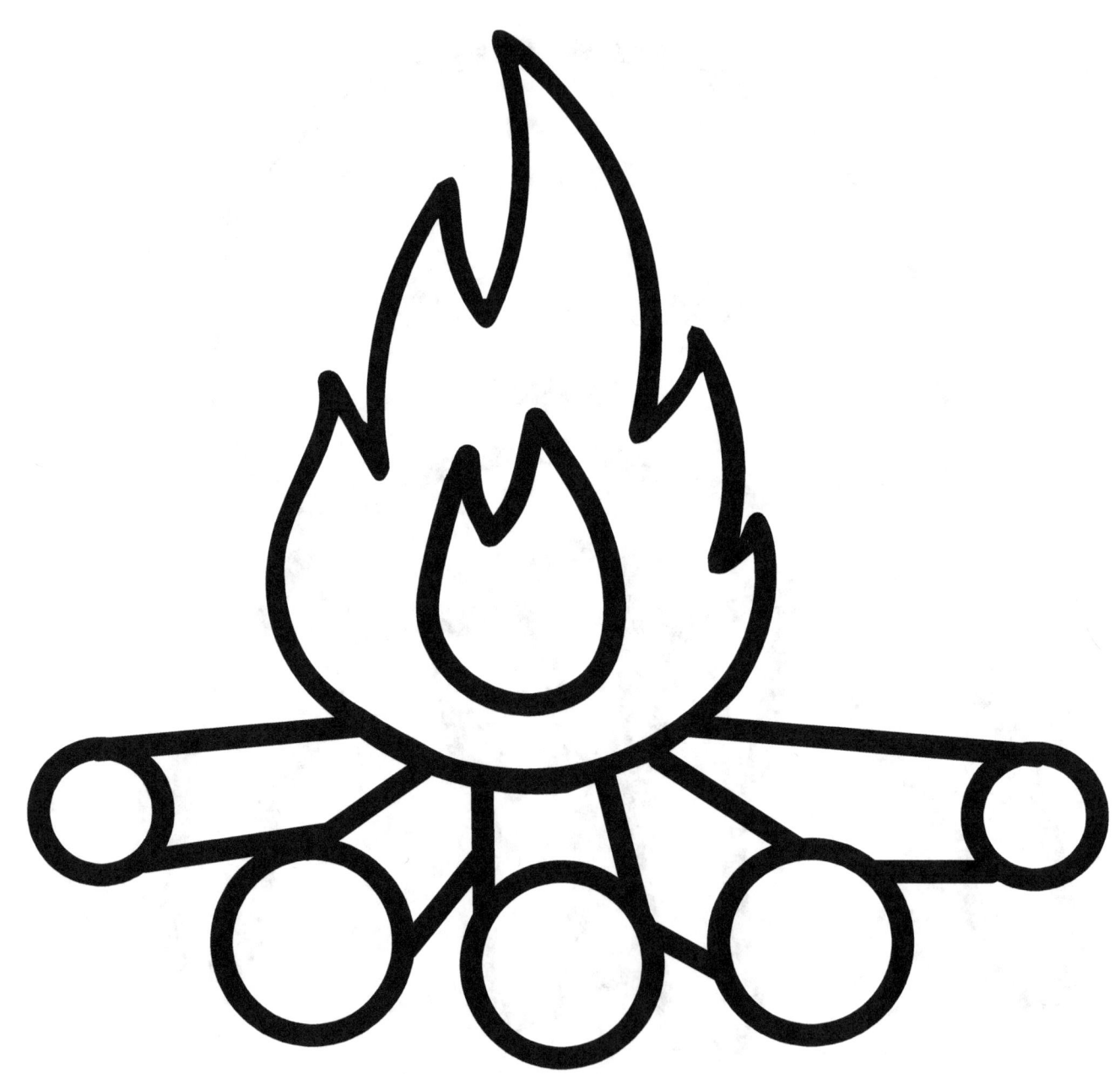

SO FUN!

The Beach

AND ME!

Are we there

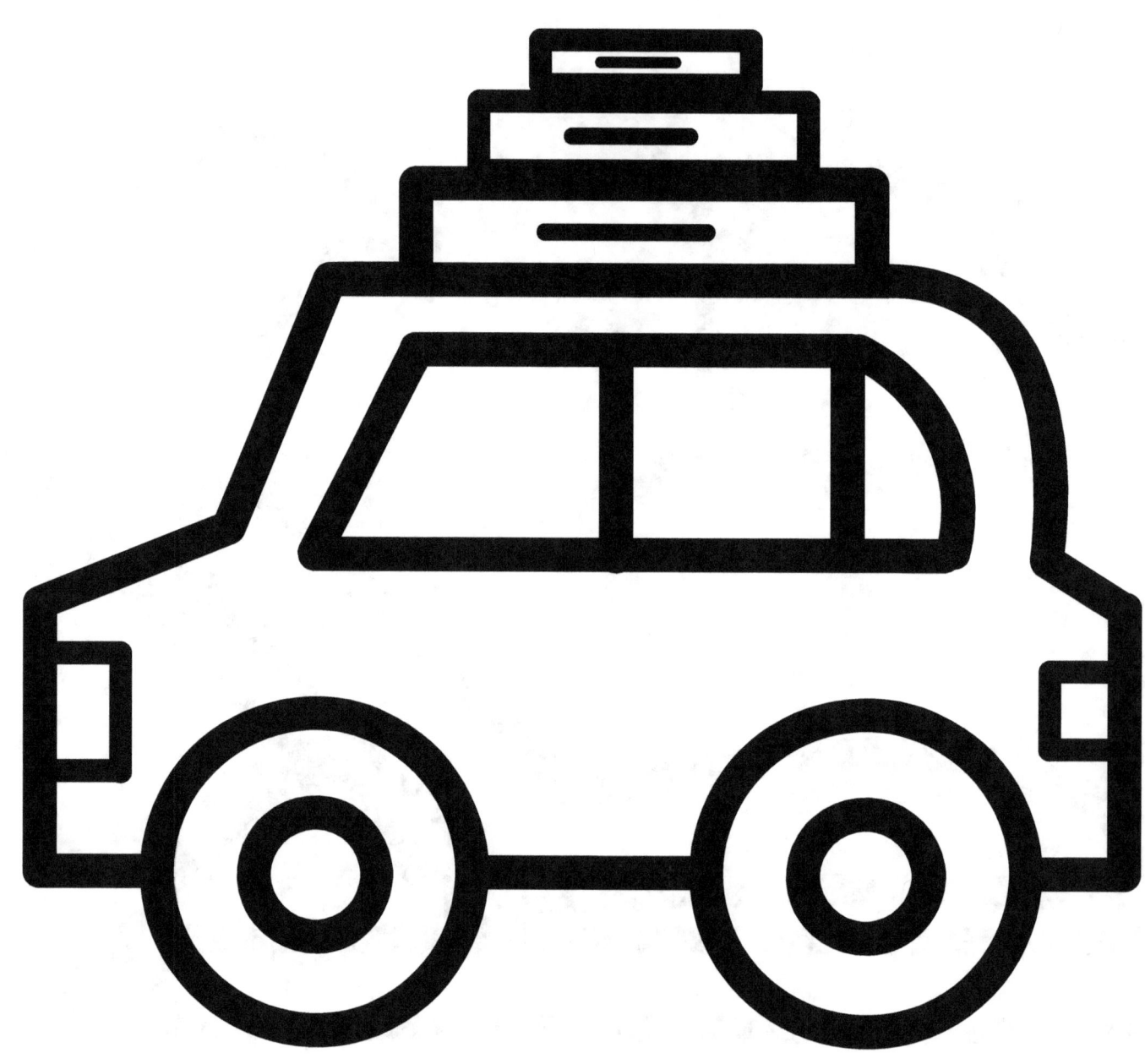

YET?

The sun is

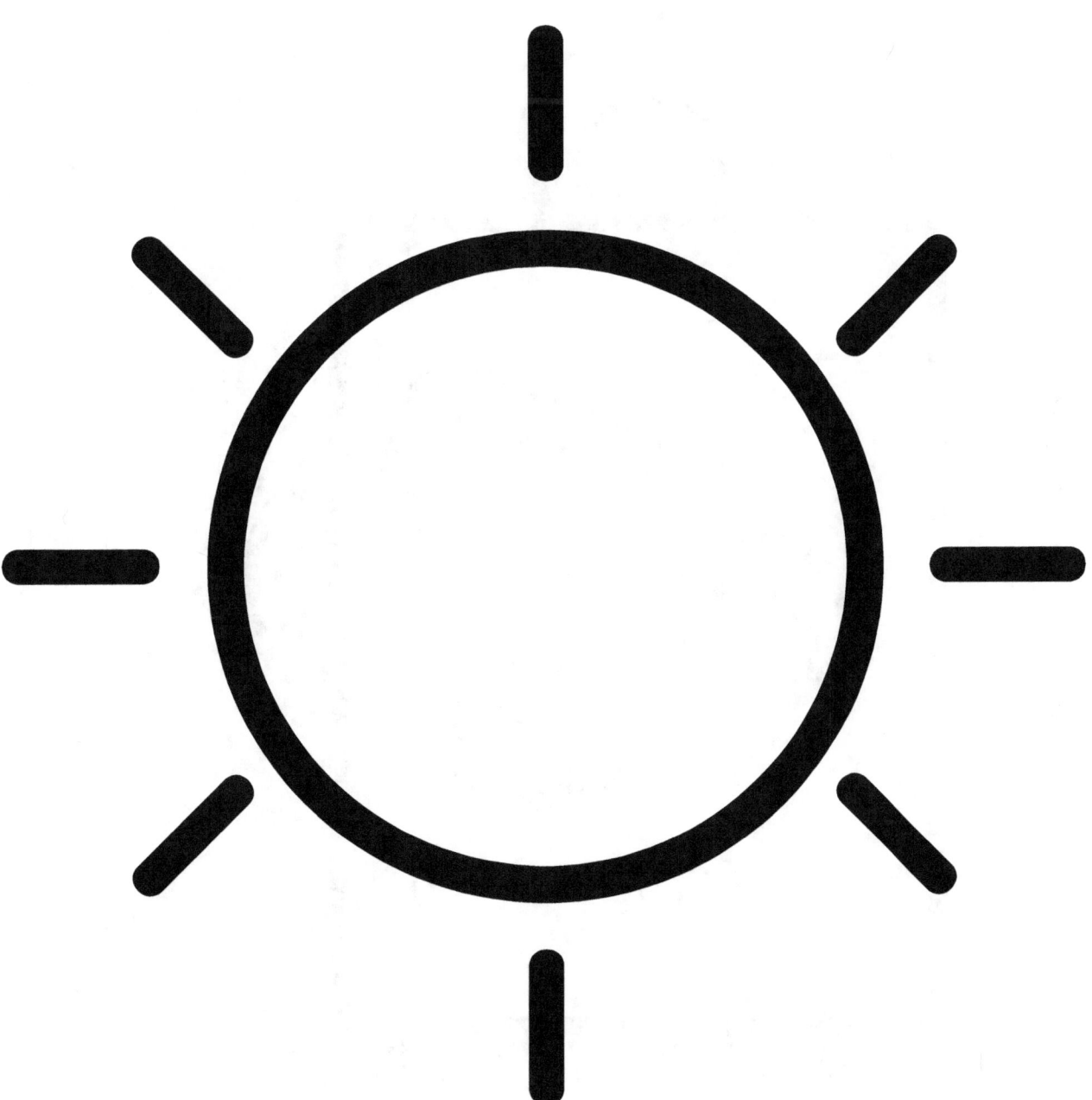

OUT!

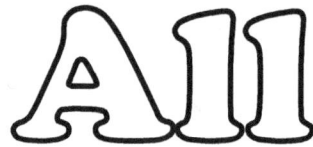

All

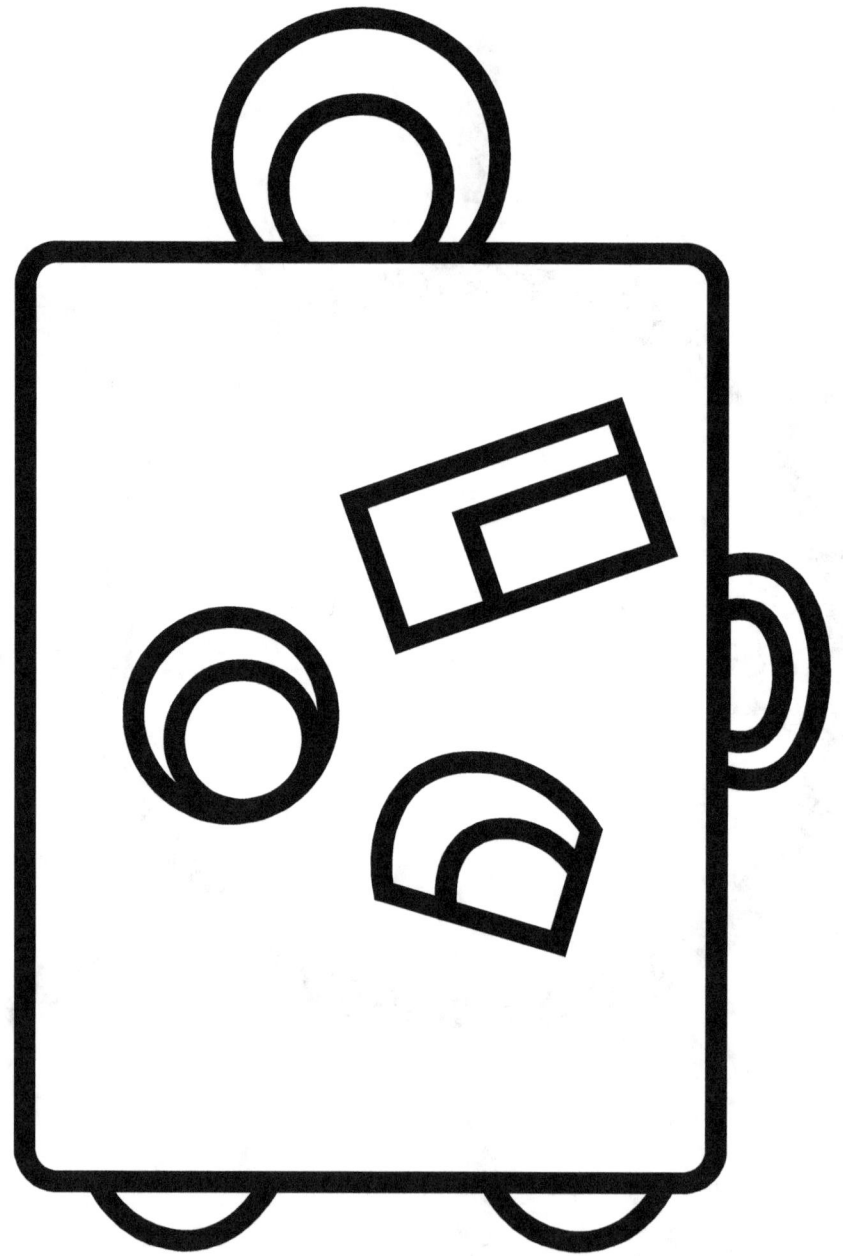

PACKED!

Safety

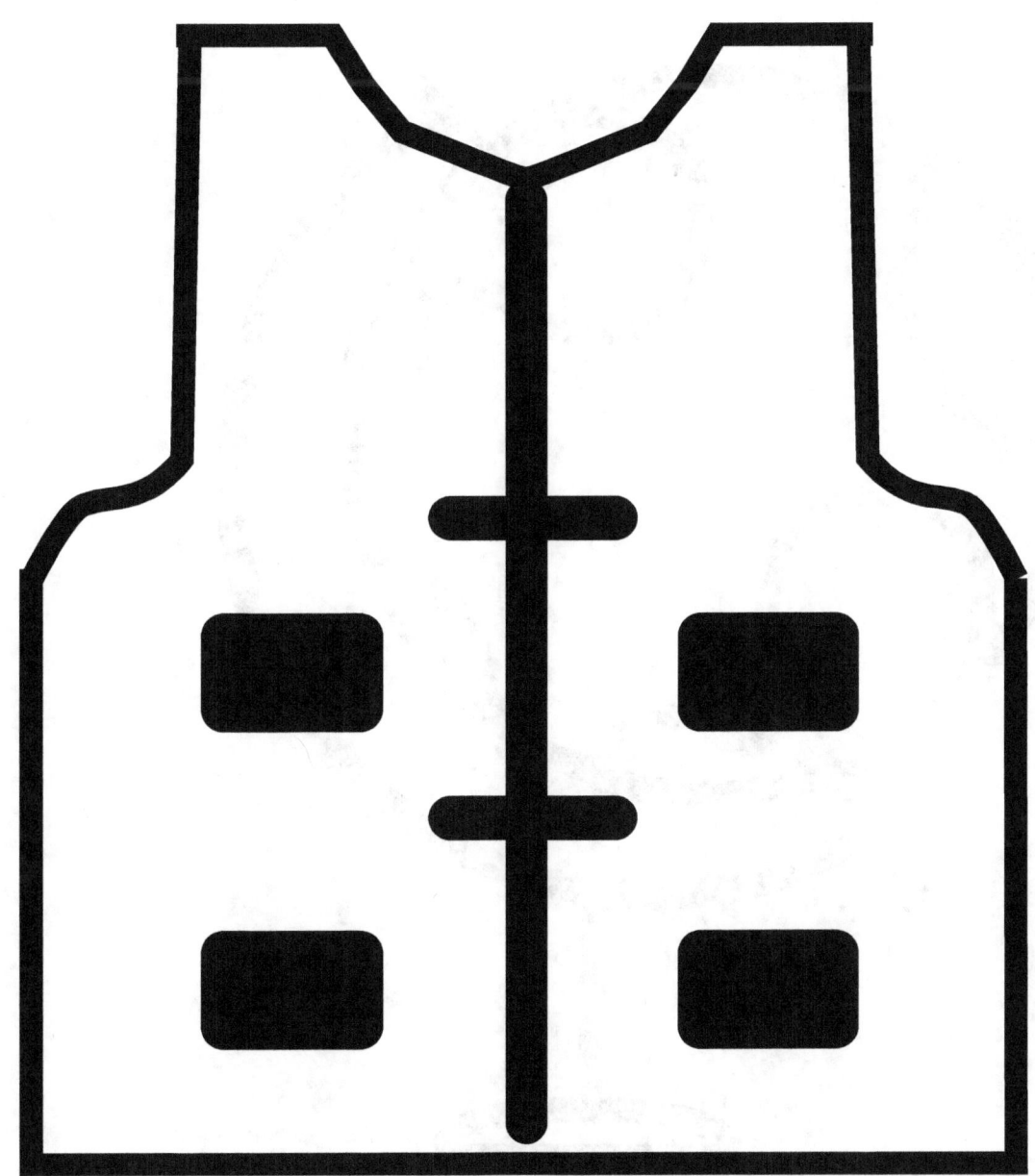

FIRST!

Watch out

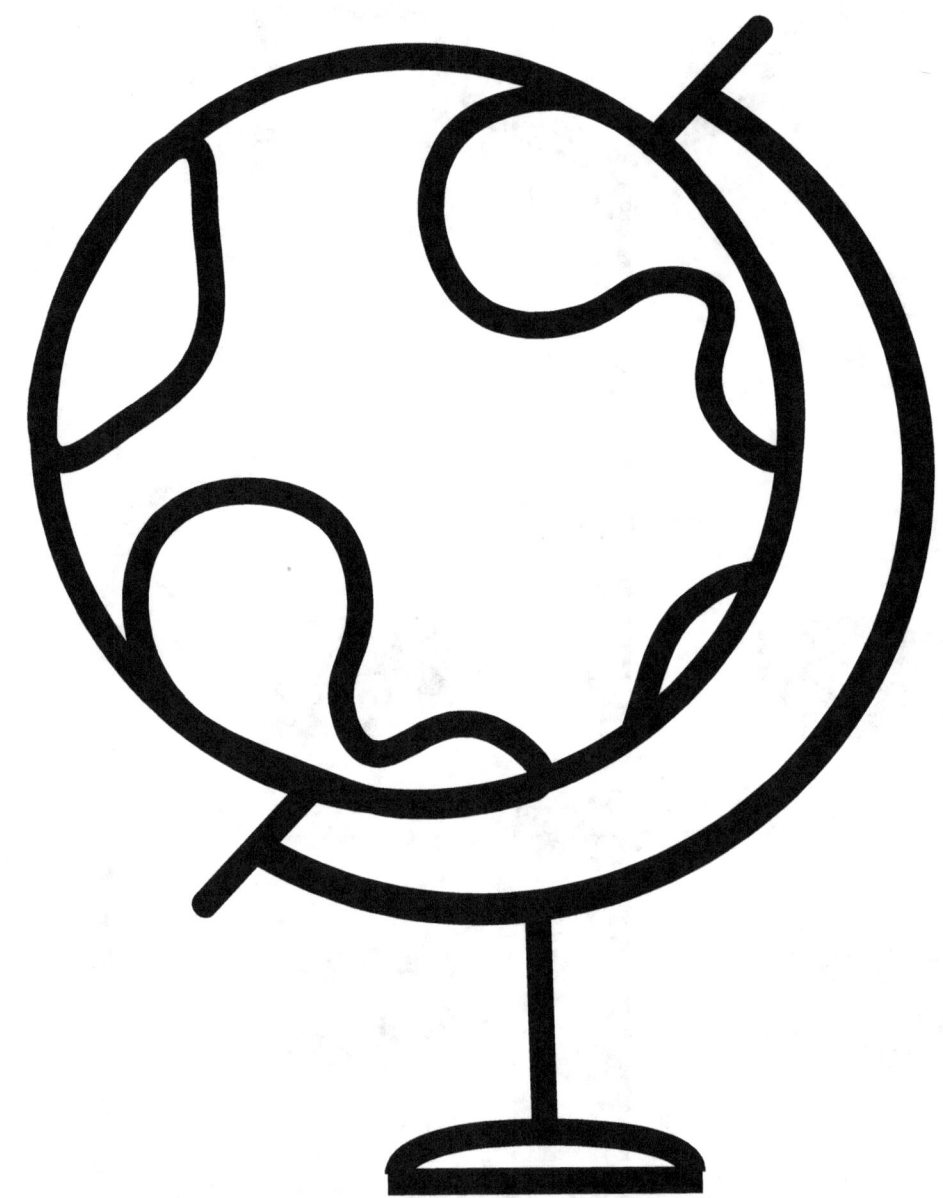

WORLD!

Let's travel

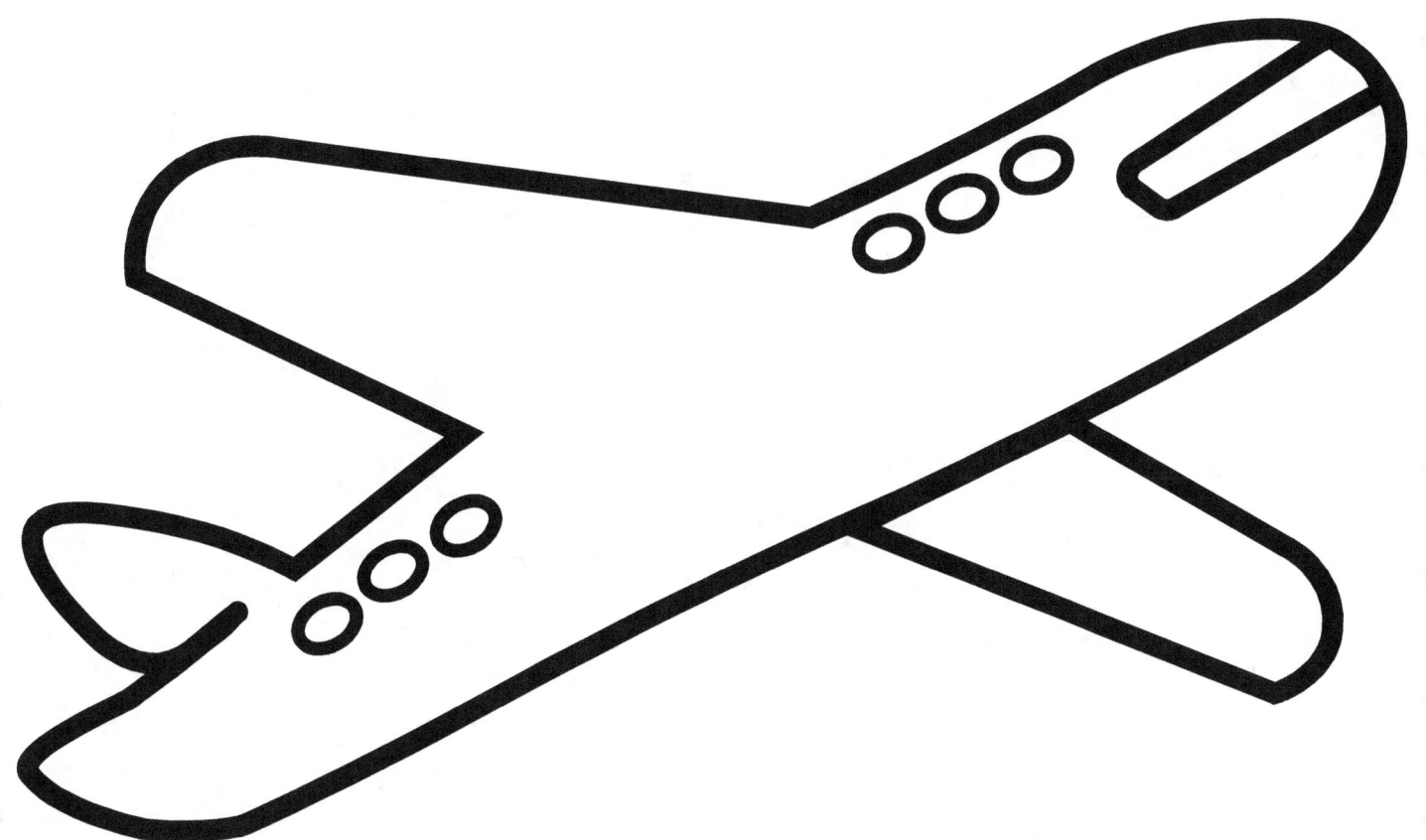

TOGETHER!

Draw a picture of your favorite Travels.

Scrap your Photo HERE